ASTROLOGY

LIBRA

BY TRUDY BECKER

Apex is distributed by North Star Editions:
sales@northstareditions.com | 888-417-0195

Produced for Apex by Red Line Editorial.

Photographs ©: Shutterstock Images, cover (illustration, constellation), cover (background), 1, 4–5, 7, 8, 10–11, 12–13, 14–15, 16–17, 18, 19, 20, 21, 22–23, 24–25, 26–27, 29; iStockphoto, 9

Library of Congress Control Number: 2025939148

ISBN
979-8-89250-786-8 (hardcover)
979-8-89250-815-5 (paperback)
979-8-89250-872-8 (ebook pdf)
979-8-89250-844-5 (hosted ebook)

Printed in the United States of America
Mankato, MN
012026

NOTE TO PARENTS AND EDUCATORS

Apex books are designed to build literacy skills in striving readers. Exciting, high-interest content attracts and holds readers' attention. The text is carefully leveled to allow students to achieve success quickly. Additional features, such as bolded glossary words for difficult terms, help build comprehension.

TABLE OF CONTENTS

CHAPTER 1

SCALES IN THE SKY

Libra is a **constellation**. Some of its stars form a triangle. Others make two lines that stick out from it.

Libra includes more than 80 stars. Six stars form the main shape.

People first saw this shape in the stars thousands of years ago. Some thought it looked like a set of scales. They called the constellation Libra. That means "weighing scales" in Latin.

FAST FACT

Ancient Sumerians called Libra "Zib-ba An-na." That means "balance of heaven."

For many years, people have used scales to weigh things when buying or selling them.

Some **myths** link Libra to Astraea. She was a Greek goddess of **justice**. She carried a set of scales.

Astraea was one of several goddesses linked with laws and justice. Some had blindfolds to show they would treat all people fairly.

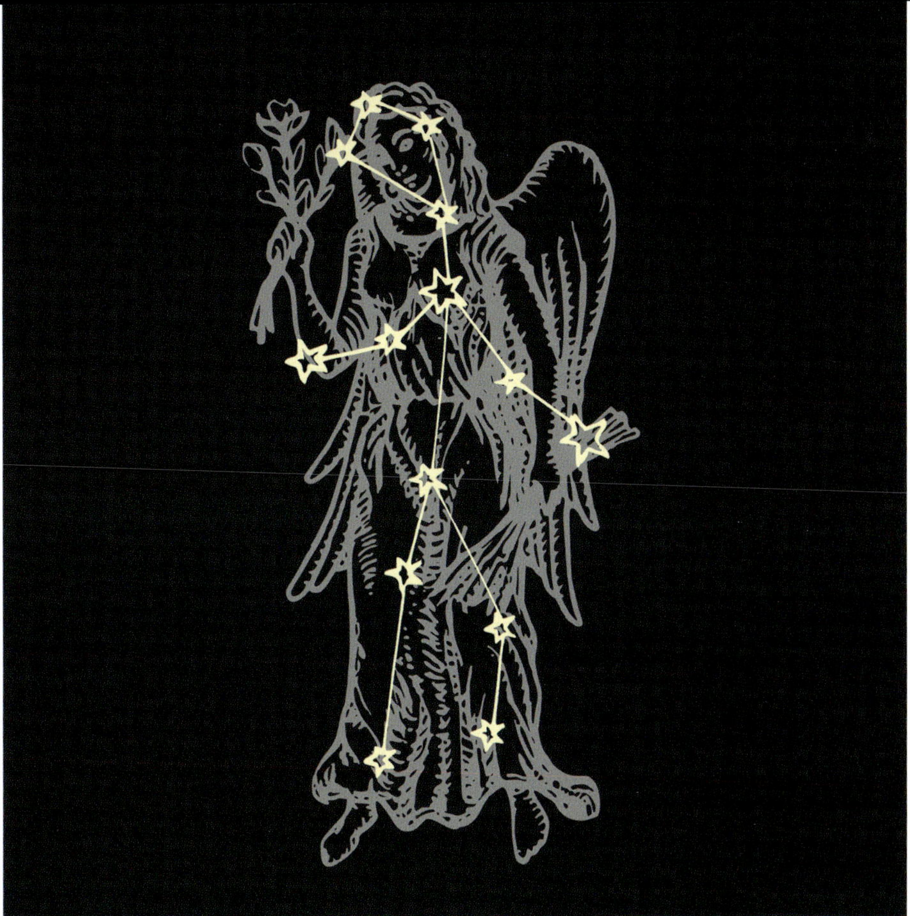

The constellation Virgo appears in the night sky near Libra.

BECOMING STARS

According to myth, Astraea once lived on Earth. But people became too wicked. So, she went up to the sky. She became the constellation Virgo. Her scales became Libra.

CHAPTER 2

THE ZODIAC

Libra is part of the **zodiac**. There are 12 zodiac signs. They split the year into 12 parts. Libra comes seventh.

Each zodiac sign is based on a different constellation.

Libra's time begins around September 23. It lasts until about October 23. People born during that period have Libra as their **sun sign**.

FAST FACT

In the northern **hemisphere**, Libra's time starts on the first day of fall.

The first day of fall has 12 hours of darkness and 12 hours of light. So, the day is often linked to balance.

Astrology claims that sun signs shape how people think and act. For example, Libras are said to be friendly and charming.

RISING SIGNS

Sun signs are a key part of astrology. But people have other signs, too. For instance, rising signs are based on the time of day people were born. They're said to shape how people show themselves to others.

A rising sign is one of 12 houses used in astrology. Each house is said to shape a different part of someone's life.

CHAPTER 3

ABOUT LIBRA

The **glyph** for Libra uses two lines. The top line has a big curve in the middle. Together, the lines look like a setting sun.

Each zodiac sign has its own glyph.

Libra's **element** is air. People with air signs are said to love thinking and talking. Libras may spend lots of time discussing ideas with friends.

The three air signs are Gemini, Libra, and Aquarius.

Many Libras love reading.

FAST FACT

People with air signs often like learning.

Libra's ruling planet is Venus. This planet is said to shape how Libras act. Venus was the Roman goddess of love and beauty. So, Libras often care a lot about relationships.

Libras may spend lots of time thinking about dating and romance.

Libras are known for having great taste. They often like art, music, and fancy food.

STYLISH SIGN

Libras often have an eye for beauty. They may be good at art or decorating. And they may like having nice things. For example, they may wear stylish clothes.

CHAPTER 4

FINDING BALANCE

Many Libras care about justice. They try to make fair choices. They often think carefully about all sides. Sometimes, they struggle to choose.

Libras may spend a long time thinking before they act.

Many Libras are good listeners. They help others feel seen and understood.

Libras also tend to be very social. They love to be around others. And they connect well with many kinds of people.

FAST FACT

Famous Libras include Jenna Ortega, Travis Kelce, and Jimin from BTS.

Libras like when things feel peaceful. They can bring peace to others, too. They help people see what they have in common, even during disagreements.

Libras tend to be good at helping others get along.

DOWNSIDES

Libras often try to make everyone happy. This sometimes causes problems. To avoid fights, Libras may just say what others want to hear. They may hide or ignore their true feelings.

COMPREHENSION QUESTIONS

Write your answers on a separate piece of paper.

1. Write a few sentences describing some ways that Libras are said to act.

2. Do you try to avoid fights? Why or why not?

3. What part of the zodiac is Libra?

- **A.** the first part
- **B.** the seventh part
- **C.** the tenth part

4. How might hiding their feelings be unhelpful for Libras?

- **A.** Other people might not know what Libras really want.
- **B.** Other people might care too much about what Libras think and feel.
- **C.** Hiding their feelings might cause Libras to not listen to others.

5. What does **discussing** mean in this book?

People with air signs are said to love thinking and talking. Libras may spend lots of time ***discussing*** *ideas with friends.*

- **A.** moving something around
- **B.** staying away from something
- **C.** speaking about something in detail

6. What does **social** mean in this book?

Libras also tend to be very ***social****. They love to be around others.*

- **A.** liking to be with other people
- **B.** liking to spend time alone
- **C.** liking to sleep in late

Answer key on page 32.

GLOSSARY

constellation
A group of stars that form a shape.

element
One of four forces (air, earth, fire, or water) that each zodiac sign is matched with and said to be shaped by.

glyph
A shape that stands for a word or idea.

hemisphere
One half of planet Earth.

justice
Doing what is right and fair.

myths
Well-known stories from the past that often include magic.

sun sign
A person's main zodiac sign, which is decided by the date they were born.

zodiac
The set of 12 signs used in astrology, based on a part of the sky that the sun appears to move through each year.

TO LEARN MORE

BOOKS

Goldstein, Margaret J. *Mysteries of Stars*. Lerner Publications, 2021.

Huddleston, Emma. *Explore the Stars*. Abdo Publishing, 2022.

McMullen, Gemma. *The Stars*. Little Blue House, 2025.

ONLINE RESOURCES

Visit **www.apexeditions.com** to find links and resources related to this title.

ABOUT THE AUTHOR

Trudy Becker lives in Minneapolis, Minnesota. She likes exploring new places and loves anything involving books.

INDEX

ANSWER KEY:
1. Answers will vary; 2. Answers will vary; 3. B; 4. A; 5. C; 6. A